THE BALANCED LIFE

UNLOCKING HAPPINESS

STEPHEN LOVETT

Published by Brolga Publishing Pty Ltd
ABN 46 063 962 443
PO Box 452
Torquay 3228 VIC
Australia

email: markzocchi@brolgapublishing.com.au

ISBN: 978-1-7640776-2-0

Printed in Australia

Cover design by Luke Harris, WorkingType Studio

Typeset by WorkingType Studio

STEVE "TOUGH LOVE" LOVETT

Boxing was my life for over half of it. In the ring, I earned the name "Tough Love" a name that reflected not just my style, but my mindset. But life outside the ring called me to grow in new directions. Through hard lessons and focused reflection, I loosened boxing's grip on me without ever letting go of its discipline and heart.

Today, I'm a devoted husband to Alexandra and a proud father to our three children our 5 year old son and 1 year old twin girls. I work with my hands as a stonemason shaping stone with the same care and precision I once brought to the gym. I still train up and coming fighters, sharing not just technique, but the deeper lessons boxing taught me.

I'm a thinker always learning, always evolving. I rise early, before the world stirs, and in that quiet, I write. It's there I reflect, explore, and reconnect with the man I'm still becoming.

www.thebalancedlife.com.au

Also by Stephen Lovett:

Tough is Not Enough, published by Brolga Publishing.

CONTENTS

Search for balance 1

Chapter 1 Understanding the Relationship Between Happiness and Financial Success 5

Chapter 2 Self Discovery: Knowing What Truly Matters 9

Chapter 3 The Power of Mindset Shifting from Scarcity to Abundance 17

Chapter 4 Financial Literacy Making Money Work for You 27

Chapter 5 Work Life Harmony Crafting a Life You Love 37

Chapter 6 Embracing Change Adapting to Evolving Needs 49

Chapter 7 Building a Legacy, Giving Back and Finding Purpose 59

Conclusion 69

The Ongoing Journey to Balance 69

Closing Story 71

SEARCH FOR BALANCE

This is something deep and universally felt, the constant juggling act we all face in life. It's almost like walking a tightrope where every step matters, and if we lean too far one way, we risk losing our balance entirely. There's always that pull between our desire to succeed in our work and make ends meet, and the equally important need to nurture our relationships, protect our health, and find time for personal joy. It's not always about the grand things but often about finding harmony in the little moments.

When we put all our energy into work, thinking we're doing it for the family, we risk sacrificing our health, relationships, and peace of mind. Yet, when we focus on our passions or loved ones, it's easy to feel the strain of financial worries or the pressure to secure our future. Both extremes have their consequences.

The key to It all might not lie in a perfect balance but in a flexible, evolving approach where we can shift priorities when needed. Sometimes, we need to make room for self-care without feeling guilty. Other times, we may need to dive into work, knowing it's part of a larger goal for the ones we love. And of course, we shouldn't forget the power of saying "no" when the demands become overwhelming.

Ultimately, finding balance could also mean embracing imperfection, recognizing that no day will ever feel like we've gotten it all right, but that's okay. It's about the consistent effort to check in with ourselves, be mindful, and make adjustments as we go along. Balance isn't something we "achieve" it's something we navigate through, step by step.

ME

Today is March 11, 2025, but let's rewind to the summer of 1998, when my life took a pivotal turn. I was just 13 years old, in year 7 at school, and that's when boxing came into my life. From that moment on, boxing became my everything.

I was playing sports mainly football and cricket, but nothing compared to the passion I found in boxing. I immersed myself completely, I read about it, watched every fight, and trained relentlessly. For the next 25 years, boxing consumed my life.

But here's the thing: I didn't realize how unbalanced my life had become. I was pouring nearly 80% of my time into boxing. The remaining time? Scattered across relationships, family, and academics. In hindsight, that lack of balance took a toll on my mental health.

I was so focused on becoming a better boxer that I neglected other important aspects of my life. It wasn't just about the sport; it was about finding harmony within myself.

Now, as I reflect on those years, I understand the importance of balance. It's vital to allocate time for your passions but equally crucial to nurture relationships and invest in your personal growth.

LIFE
WORK
HEALTH

CHAPTER 1

Understanding the Relationship Between Happiness and Financial Success

Have you ever stopped to wonder about the true cost of chasing money? Not just the physical or emotional effort but what it does to your relationships, your peace of mind, your day to day joy. In a world where success is often measured by the size of your bank account or the brand of your car, it's easy to get swept away in the illusion that more money equals more happiness.

Sure, financial security matters. It can provide stability, open doors to opportunities, and allow us to support those we care about. But when the desire for wealth becomes an obsession when it becomes the central goal of our lives it can blind us to the things that truly enrich our existence.

We often believe that having plenty of cash will grant us freedom the freedom to do what we want, go where we please, and buy whatever our hearts desire. But let's pause for a moment. Is that really happiness? Or is it just comfort wrapped in expensive packaging?

In the pursuit of wealth, many of us dive headfirst into a mindset where making money becomes our sole focus. We convince ourselves that once we "make it," we'll finally be able to relax and enjoy life. But that finish line keeps moving. The more we earn, the more we want. Ambition turns into a treadmill always running, never arriving.

Meanwhile, the things that bring deep, lasting fulfillment like love, friendship, laughter, creativity, and peace slowly slip through our fingers. We work longer hours, bring stress home, and cut corners on sleep and self-care. We stop showing up fully for the people who matter most. Our children grow up while we're buried in our laptops. Our friendships fade. Our passions sit neglected in the corners of our lives.

Sure, you can buy the latest phone or book that dream vacation. But what's the point if you're too exhausted to enjoy it? And who are you sharing those moments with? The joy of life isn't found in possessions it's found in connection.

When we focus solely on accumulating wealth, we risk losing the very things that give our lives meaning. The cost isn't always visible it's emotional and spiritual. You can have millions in the bank and still feel hollow inside. You can be surrounded by luxury and still feel alone.

This is where balance becomes not just helpful but essential. True success lies in finding that sweet spot where financial well.being coexists with emotional and relational health. You can have a thriving career and still make time for the people and activities that light you up. You don't have to sacrifice your joy on the altar of financial gain.

The good news? It's absolutely possible to build a life that includes both prosperity and peace. It starts by redefining what success means to you. Is it the number in your bank account? Or is it waking up with purpose, going to bed with gratitude, and filling your days with people and experiences that matter?

In this journey toward a more meaningful life, we'll explore practical strategies for creating wealth without sacrificing happiness. From developing healthier work habits to nurturing emotional intelligence and setting clear values based goals, we'll look at how you can thrive in every area not just financially.

Because you deserve both: a life of abundance and a life of joy.

Remember, life isn't just about making money, it's about enjoying the journey with those you love by your side. Let's begin to shift the narrative, moving from the constant hustle to a more holistic vision of success one rooted in balance, intention, and genuine fulfillment.

So, join me as we take this first step toward reclaiming your happiness without letting go of your ambitions. Let's discover what it really means to live well.

CHAPTER 2

Self Discovery: Knowing What Truly Matters

Have you ever paused really paused to think about what brings you joy and fulfillment beyond the numbers in your bank account? In a world that constantly pushes us to define ourselves by what we do, what we own, or how much we earn, the deeper questions often get drowned out by noise. But here's a truth that many of us forget: until you know what truly matters to you, success of any kind will feel empty.

Self discovery isn't just some vague, feel good concept. It's the bedrock of a meaningful, intentional life. When you know who you are and what you value, you stop drifting. You begin steering your life with clarity and confidence. You no longer make decisions based on fear, approval, or habit you make them from a place of truth.

How do you begin this journey?

Start with Stillness

Let's begin with something simple yet powerful: journaling. Set aside just ten minutes a day maybe in the morning before the world rushes in or at night when things are quiet. Ask yourself:

"When did I last feel truly happy?"

Write about the moment. What were you doing? Who were you with? How did your body feel light, energized, calm? These small reflections, done consistently, begin to paint a picture of your inner world. Over time, you'll notice patterns emerge clues pointing you toward what genuinely fulfills you.

Next, try a mindfulness practice. You don't need a fancy cushion or a perfect technique. Just find a quiet space, close your eyes, and take slow, deep breaths. Then gently ask yourself:

"What makes my heart sing?"

Let the answers come without judgment. Maybe it's spending time in nature. Maybe it's teaching, building, creating, or nurturing. When we create space for inner listening, we begin to hear the voice we've been ignoring our own.

The Power of Simplification: Marie's Story

A few years ago, Marie's life looked "successful" on the outside: a stable job, a nice home, a calendar packed with events. But inside, she felt overwhelmed. Her home was cluttered with things she rarely used, and her days were filled with obligations that didn't align with her passions. Every morning felt heavy. Every night, she was drained.

One weekend, after a particularly stressful week, she made a bold decision: to simplify not just her space, but her life.

She started small. Her closet. Clothes she hadn't worn in years gone. Then came the kitchen, the shelves, the garage. But what began as a physical purge quickly turned inward. Marie started asking, "Why am

I holding on to things that don't serve me physically, mentally, emotionally?"

She stepped back from draining relationships. She stopped overcommitting. She unfollowed accounts that made her feel inadequate. And in the quiet space that followed, something unexpected happened she remembered her dream of starting her own design business.

With fewer distractions and more clarity, Marie slowly built that dream. Her minimalist lifestyle became her brand clean lines, intentional choices, meaningful designs. Within a year, she wasn't just thriving creatively she was earning more than she had at her previous job. But most importantly, she felt whole.

Marie's story teaches us that decluttering isn't just about your closet it's about clearing the path to your truth.

Taking Action: Tools and Practices

If you're not sure where to start, try a few of these practical steps:

Career assessments: These can help you identify your strengths, interests, and values. Sometimes we need objective tools to uncover parts of ourselves we've forgotten.

Mindful routines: A walk in nature. A morning cup of tea enjoyed without distraction. A few moments of gratitude before bed. These small practices anchor us to the present and to ourselves.

Boundaries: Say no to things that don't align with your values. Time is your most precious resource spend it on what matters.

Digital declutter: Unfollow accounts, mute notifications, unsubscribe from emails that clutter your mental space.

The Compass Within

Self discovery means asking hard questions and being willing to hear the answers.

- **What do I value most in life?**
- **What kind of relationships do I want to cultivate?**
- **What kind of legacy do I want to leave?**

These aren't questions with quick answers. But the more you sit with them, the clearer your path becomes.

When you live in alignment with your core values, you stop chasing happiness and start creating it. Your life begins to feel more like your own. The opinions of others lose their grip. The pressure to keep up fades. And what remains is peace a deep, quiet knowing that you are exactly where you're meant to be.

The Reward of Knowing Yourself

Finding yourself isn't just a trendy phrase it's the heart of happiness. When you know who you are, everything changes. Your goals become clearer. Your relationships deepen. Your decisions become easier.

You stop measuring success by someone else's yardstick. You define it on your own terms.

And here's the magic: when you're living authentically, opportunities flow more naturally. You attract the right people, the right work, and the right kind of abundance. Happiness stops being a distant goal it becomes the byproduct of a life lived in truth.

So, take a moment today to check in with yourself. Reflect. Write. Breathe. Ask the tough questions. You might be surprised at what rises to the surface.

Self-discovery isn't always easy but it's always worth it.

Because once you know what truly matters, you'll never settle for less again.

SELF-DISCOVERY
KNOWING WHAT MATTERS
VALUES

CHAPTER 3

The Power of Mindset Shifting from Scarcity to Abundance

Have you ever felt like no matter how hard you try, you're always just one step behind? Like there's never quite enough money, time, opportunity, love? That quiet, anxious whisper inside that says, "You're not enough... and there's not enough to go around." That's the scarcity mindset at work.

The scarcity mindset is more than just occasional doubt it's a deep rooted belief system that convinces us we're operating in a world of limitation. It tells us to hoard, to fear, to compare. It makes us believe that if someone else wins, we must lose. That if we don't grab what we can now, there might not be another chance.

And perhaps most dangerously, it leads us to shrink ourselves, our dreams, our ambitions, and our sense of self worth because we're afraid we're not enough to begin with.

But here's the truth: you can shift this mindset. It's not set in stone. You have the power to retrain your thoughts and beliefs. You can move from scarcity to abundance from fear to possibility, from limitation to expansion.

What is the Abundance Mindset?

The abundance mindset doesn't mean ignoring reality or pretending challenges don't exist. It means choosing to believe that even in the face of difficulty, possibility remains. That there is enough, enough opportunity, enough success, enough joy to go around. It's the belief that your worth is not determined by circumstances, and that growth is always available to you.

When you adopt this mindset, your entire life begins to shift. Instead of viewing others as competition, you begin to see them as collaborators. Instead of feeling jealousy when someone succeeds, you feel inspired because their success reminds you of what's possible for you too.

Start with Gratitude

Gratitude is the simplest, most powerful tool for rewiring your mind.

Each morning, take a few minutes to write down three things you're grateful for. They don't have to be big a warm cup of coffee, a kind text from a friend, the sound of birds outside your window. This practice shifts your focus away from what's missing to what's present. And over time, your brain will begin to look for the good automatically.

Gratitude softens fear and sharpens clarity. It makes room for abundance to take root.

Affirmations That Build Belief

Your words have power especially the ones you say to yourself.

If your inner dialogue is full of phrases like,. "I'll never have enough," "I'm not good with money," or "Success isn't for people like me," it's time to flip the script.

Use affirmations to plant new beliefs. Say them out loud. Write them down. Feel them in your body.

"I am worthy of wealth and well-being."

"Opportunities are always flowing toward me."

"There is more than enough for me and everyone else."

"I trust that everything I need is already on its way."

These aren't magic words - they are mental habits. And like any habit, the more you practice them, the more real they become.

Reframing: Turning Fear into Fuel

When a negative thought shows up, don't ignore it engage with it. Ask, "Is this thought helping or hurting me?" Most of the time, our limiting thoughts are outdated survival mechanisms, not current truths.

Reframe them:

Instead of "I'll never get out of debt," try "I'm learning to make smarter financial choices each day."

Instead of "I'm not as successful as others," try "I'm on my own path, and I honor its timing."

Reframing doesn't mean lying to yourself. It means choosing an empowering perspective over a defeating one.

Real-Life Inspiration: The Story of Oprah Winfrey

If there's anyone who embodies the shift from scarcity to abundance, it's Oprah.

Born into poverty, raised in a troubled home, and faced with trauma from an early age, Oprah's story could have been defined by limitation. But she didn't let her past dictate her future. Instead of clinging to a scarcity narrative, she cultivated a deep sense of self-worth and possibility.

She immersed herself in books. She dreamed big. She believed fiercely that she was meant for more. And even when doors slammed in her face, she didn't shrink. She rose.

Today, Oprah isn't just one of the most influential women in the world she's a living example of abundance in action. Her success, generosity, and grace are rooted not in luck, but in mindset.

Your Turn: Stepping Into Abundance

Here's how you can begin shifting your own mindset today:

1. Daily Gratitude Practice: Write down three things you're grateful for every morning or evening. Let them be specific and meaningful.

2. Affirmations Routine: Choose 2-3 affirmations that resonate with you. Say them aloud in the mirror daily especially when doubt creeps in.

3. Mindset Check-Ins: Throughout the day, notice your thoughts. When scarcity shows up, pause and ask, "What would an abundance mindset say here?"

4. Celebrate Others: Practice abundance by celebrating other people's wins instead of comparing yourself. Their success is not your failure it's proof that big things are possible.

5. Visualize Growth: Spend a few minutes visualizing the life you want how it feels, how it looks, how you show up in it. Anchor yourself in that feeling of expansion.

Scarcity keeps you small. Abundance invites you to grow.

You get to choose which lens you use to view the world. One keeps you stuck in fear. The other opens you to a life of possibility.

Look around. There is enough. You are enough. And your journey unique, imperfect, beautiful is unfolding exactly as it should.

Step into abundance. Your future is waiting.

FINANCIAL LITERACY
MAKING MONEY WORK FOR YOU
BUDGETING
INCOME
EXPENSES
RENT
FOOD
TRANSPORT
SAVING
EMERGENCY FUND
SAVE EARLY
COMPOUND INTEREST
DEBT
SMALL DEBT
FINANCIAL
LITERACY
SMART CHOICES
SNOWBALL METHOD
FIRE MOVEMENT
FIRE
FINANCIAL INDEPENDENCE, RETIRE EARLY
MAKE MONEY WORK FOR YOU
START TODAY · YOUR FUTURE SELF WILL THANK YOU!

CHAPTER 4

Financial Literacy Making Money Work for You

Have you ever felt overwhelmed by money where it goes, how to grow it, or how to stop stressing over it? You're not alone. Most of us were never taught how to manage our finances in a meaningful way. Yet financial literacy is one of the most powerful life skills you can cultivate. It's not just about crunching numbers it's about creating a life of choice, freedom, and intention.

Financial literacy puts you in the driver's seat of your life. When you understand how money works, you stop chasing it and start directing it. As John D. Rockefeller wisely said:

"He who works all day has no time to make money."

In other words, wealth isn't just built by hard work it's built by smart decisions.

Let's break it down step by step. Because when you understand the basics, you build a foundation for financial peace and ultimately, a life you truly love.

1. Budgeting: Telling Your Money Where to Go

A budget isn't about restriction it's about clarity.

Think of budgeting as your financial GPS. It shows you where you are and helps you get to where you want to go. Without it, it's easy to lose track of spending, fall into debt, or wonder why you're working so hard with little to show for it.

Start with these simple steps:

Track your income: Know exactly how much you bring in each month.

List your expenses: Include everything rent, mortgage, food, bills, subscriptions, transportation, and fun money.

Create categories: Use the 50/30/20 rule as a starting point:

- 50% on needs (housing, utilities, groceries)
- 30% on wants (entertainment, eating out)
- 20% on savings and debt repayment

2. Saving: Building Your Safety Net

Saving money is about more than having a cushion it's about peace of mind. Life throws curveballs. A car repair, a job loss, a medical emergency. When you have savings, you don't spiral you stay steady.

Aim to save at least 20% of your income if possible, but start with whatever you can even 5%. Small amounts add up, especially when saved consistently.

Here's how to get started:

- Emergency Fund: Build a fund with 3-6 months' worth of living expenses. Keep it in a high yield savings account where it's accessible but growing.
- Automate It: Set up automatic transfers so you "pay yourself first" before spending on anything else.

Every dollar saved is a vote for your future security.

3. Investing: Letting Your Money Grow

Investing isn't just for the wealthy it's for anyone who wants to stop trading time for money.

Thanks to compound interest, the earlier you start investing, the more powerful your money becomes. Consider this: $100 invested monthly at 8% annual return becomes over $150,000 in 30 years. The key is time and consistency.

Here are simple ways to start:

- Start Small: Even $25–$50 per month adds up.
- Remember: investing is a long game. Don't wait for the "perfect moment" just begin.

4. Managing Debt: Freeing Yourself from Financial Burdens

Debt is like a silent thief it steals your future income and peace of mind. But with the right plan, you can take control and eliminate it.

Start with these steps:

- List all your debts: Include balances, minimum payments, and interest rates.
- Pay off high interest debt first: Credit cards often charge 12-20% interest. That's money you could be saving or investing.

Use a method:

- Snowball: Pay off the smallest debts first for motivation.
- Avalanche: Pay off highest interest debts first to save the most money.

Either method works as long as you stay consistent. The goal is freedom.

5. Spending with Intention: Aligning Money with Values

Financial literacy isn't just about earning and saving it's about using money in ways that reflect what matters most to you.

Ask yourself:

- What experiences do I value?
- What goals matter more than stuff?
- Does this purchase support the life I want to create?

For some, it's travel. For others, education, family time, or creative freedom. Your budget should reflect your values, not just your expenses.

6. Real Life Example: The FIRE Movement

The FIRE movement Financial Independence, Retire Early isn't about escaping work. It's about designing your life around freedom and purpose.

People in this community aggressively save and invest 50-70% of their income, live below their means, and retire decades early not to do nothing, but to do what matters.

They understand a key truth:
Financial freedom = life freedom.

When your money works for you, you get to choose how to spend your time.

Even if you don't want to retire early, adopting FIRE principles like mindful spending and smart investing can change your life dramatically.

The Bigger Picture: You Are in Control

Financial literacy isn't about being perfect with money it's about being empowered. When you understand how money works, you stop fearing it. You stop avoiding your bank account. You start planning, dreaming, building.

It's never too late to start. Whether you're earning a little or a lot, you have the ability to shape your financial future. Start where you are. Learn as you go. Adjust along the way.

Because the real goal of money isn't just wealth it's freedom.

Freedom to live, to give, to rest, to explore, to be present.

Take Action Today:

- Track your spending for 30 days no judgment, just awareness.
- Start a savings account even if it's just $10/week.
- Set a goal to pay off one debt this year.

Your money doesn't define you but how you use it can shape the life you live.

Start investing in yourself financially, emotionally, and mentally and watch how everything begins to shift.

Your future self will thank you.

CHAPTER 5

Work Life Harmony
Crafting a Life You Love

It's time to challenge one of the most deeply embedded beliefs in modern culture:

"Work hard, play hard."

We've been told that success demands sacrifice that grinding for long hours is the price of achievement, and that balance is a luxury reserved for later in life. But what if that mindset is not only outdated, but harmful?

Work-life harmony,

This isn't about perfect balance or splitting your time evenly. It's about creating a rhythm where your work supports your life, not consumes it. It's about designing a life where your career fuels your energy, passion, and purpose instead of draining them.

Imagine a life where your job energizes you. Where you wake up excited, not exhausted. Where there's space to breathe, grow, connect, and create. That's not a dream it's a choice. And it starts with a shift in how you view success.

Why Work Life Harmony Matters

The old model of hustle culture glorified burnout. The badge of honor was being the busiest person in the room, checking emails at midnight, and sacrificing everything for that next promotion. But here's the reality: burnout isn't a status symbol it's a warning sign.

Work-life harmony is about sustainability. It's about aligning your work with your values and allowing space for all the other parts of you: the friend, the parent, the artist, the athlete, the dreamer.

Because you are more than your job title. And your life deserves more than leftover energy.

1. Set Clear Boundaries

Boundaries aren't just about saying "no" to others they're about saying "yes" to yourself.

Start by establishing dedicated work hours, even if you work from home or freelance. When the clock strikes five or whatever your cutoff is shut the laptop. Don't check emails. Don't take "just one more call." This physical and mental break signals your brain: Now, I rest. Now, I live.

Other boundary practices include:

- Turning off work notifications during personal time
- Setting "do not disturb" hours on your phone
- Having a separate workspace to mentally separate work and home

These boundaries protect your energy and your sanity.

2. Schedule Downtime Like It Matters because it does.

You wouldn't skip a business meeting, so why skip rest?

Downtime isn't laziness. It's recovery. It's the time when your brain recharges, your body restores, and your creativity refuels.

Try these simple recharging rituals:

- **Micro breaks**: 5-10 minutes every hour to stretch, breathe, or step outside
- **Digital detox**: One screen free hour per day to be fully present
- **Midday reset**: A short walk, quick meditation, or moment of silence between tasks

These moments may seem small, but they create a massive difference in your focus, energy, and emotional well-being.

3. Prioritize Joyful Hobbies

You are not a machine.

To feel alive, you need space for joy, play, and passion. Whether it's painting, gardening, rock climbing, journaling, or baking hobbies remind you that life is not just about productivity. They connect you with your identity beyond your profession.

Even just 30 minutes a few times a week can make a major difference in your overall happiness and motivation.

Bonus

When you feed your creativity and joy, you become more innovative and productive at work. It's a win-win.

4. Nurture Meaningful Relationships

No level of career success is worth loneliness.

Relationships are essential to resilience. They provide support when things are tough, joy when life is good, and perspective when you're stuck. And yet, they're often the first thing to get neglected when work gets busy.

Make time for the people who matter. Schedule it like any other priority:

- Weekly coffee with a friend
- Family dinner with no phones
- Monthly date night
- Weekend phone calls to loved ones

Connection fuels the soul and strengthens your sense of purpose.

5. Learn from Those Who've Done It Differently

Take inspiration from people like Tim Ferriss, author of The 4-Hour Workweek. Instead of accepting the default path of working 40+ hours a week until retirement, Tim asked, What if I designed a life that I actually loved now?

He outsourced low value tasks, streamlined his business, and reclaimed his time for what mattered: travel, learning, relationships, and wellness. His point wasn't that everyone should work four hours a week but that we all have the power to design our days intentionally.

You don't need to be an entrepreneur to live this way. Whether you're a teacher, a nurse, a manager, or a freelancer you can make choices that move you closer to harmony.

6. Redefine Success

The real shift happens when you redefine what success means to you.

Ask yourself:

- Is my current lifestyle supporting or sabotaging my well-being?
- Am I trading health and happiness for a paycheck I don't even enjoy?
- What would a fulfilling life look like, day to day?

Maybe success means flexibility. Maybe it's being able to pick your kids up from school. Maybe it's having time to write, to rest, to travel. Whatever it is honor it. Claim it. Shape your life around it.

Take Action: Craft Your Harmony Plan

Here's how to get started today:

Audit your time: Track your work and personal hours for one week. Are they balanced? Are you spending time on what truly matters?

- **Create non negotiables**: Choose 2-3 things that protect your peace daily walks, dinner with family, no emails after 7pm.
- **Design your ideal day**: Imagine a day that feels energizing, balanced, and joyful. Then take small steps toward making it real.
- **Communicate boundaries**: Let coworkers, clients, or family know what you need. Harmony starts with honesty.

You Deserve More Than the Grind

You weren't made to hustle until burnout. You were made to create, connect, and thrive.

- Work is part of life not the whole story. When you build a life that honors your needs, passions, and people, you don't just survive you shine.
- So don't wait for the perfect time to find balance. Create it now. Craft a life where your career supports your well being, where your joy matters, and where your days feel like your own.
- Because true success isn't just about what you achieve it's about how you feel while achieving it.

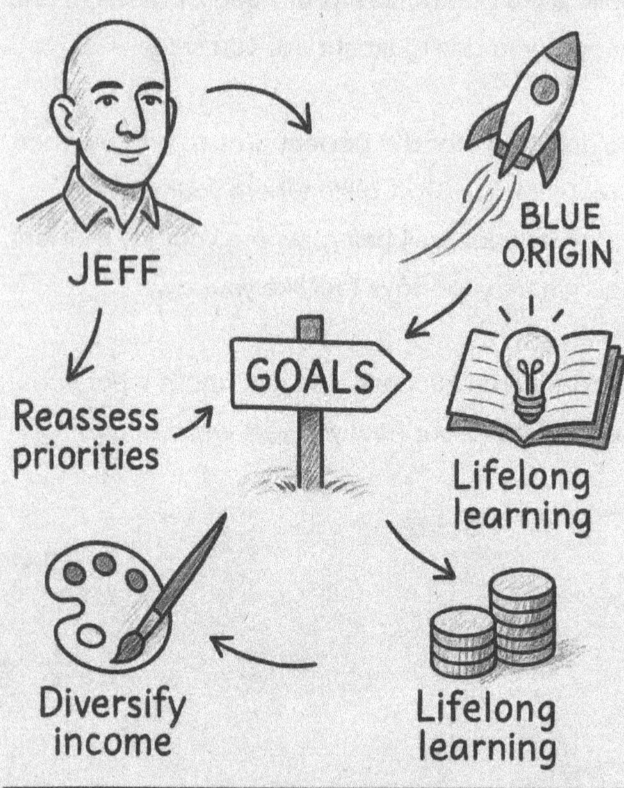
EMBRACING CHANGE
—ADAPTING TO EVOLVING NEEDS
JEFF
BLUE ORIGIN
GOALS
Reassess priorities
Lifelong learning
Diversify income
Lifelong learning
STAY FLEXIBLE AND FOCUS ON WHAT MAKES YOU HAPPY

CHAPTER 6

Embracing Change Adapting to Evolving Needs

If there's one constant in life, it's change. As we move through the seasons of our lives, our priorities, goals, and even definitions of success naturally shift. What once felt urgent or essential may lose its power over time, replaced by new desires, responsibilities, or insights. To live a fulfilled life both financially and personally we must learn to not only accept this evolution, but embrace it.

Flexibility is not a weakness. It's a superpower.

In a world that changes faster than ever before technologically, economically, and emotionally those who thrive are those who can adapt. Financial literacy and goal-setting are powerful tools, but without the ability to pivot as life unfolds, they can become outdated roadmaps.

The goal isn't to stick rigidly to one path. It's to stay aligned with what matters now and to let your money, time, and energy reflect that.

The Power of Personal Evolution

Think about your own life. What were your biggest goals five or ten years ago? Are they still the same?

Maybe you once prioritized building a career and climbing the corporate ladder. Now, you value time with family, creative freedom, or health more than professional accolades. Maybe retirement once seemed like a distant dream, but now it's a major priority.

These changes aren't failures they're signs of growth. And your financial strategy should evolve with them.

A Real-World Example: Jeff Bezos

Consider how Jeff Bezos shifted his focus over time. In the early years of Amazon, his mission was singular: build a revolutionary online bookstore, then a retail empire.

But as his company matured, so did he. Bezos began exploring new ventures that reflected his evolving interests and purpose like space exploration through Blue Origin and global sustainability efforts. This wasn't just about making more money. It was about expanding into the next chapter of his life's mission.

His journey illustrates a universal truth: true success comes from aligning your efforts with your current passions, not your past priorities.

How to Adapt with Purpose

So how do we embrace change without losing our sense of direction? Here are practical steps to keep your life and finances aligned as you evolve:

1. Reassess Your Goals Regularly

Your financial and life goals should never be "set and forget." As your needs shift whether due to family changes, career moves, or personal growth your strategy should shift too.

Action Step:

Set a yearly "life audit." Ask yourself:

- What still excites me?
- What feels outdated or draining?
- Where do I want to grow in the next 12 months?

Then update your financial plan to match. This might mean saving for travel instead of a new car, investing more in education than in luxury, or focusing on flexibility rather than status.

2. Diversify Your Income and Opportunities

Flexibility isn't just about your mindset it's also about your resources. When you rely on a single income stream, you limit your options. But when you build multiple streams side businesses, investments, freelance work, or royalties you gain freedom.

Diversified income gives you options. And options are the foundation of a life that can adapt.

Action Step:

Explore one new source of income this year. Start small. Think:

- Renting out a spare room
- Monetizing a skill or hobby
- Starting a part-time consulting gig

Even modest streams can build a foundation for future freedom.

3. Commit to Lifelong Learning

The world is changing. Fast. And to keep up, we must keep learning.

Whether you're switching careers at 40, learning about retirement planning at 60, or picking up digital skills at 25, education is empowerment. It builds confidence and keeps you agile able to pivot into new industries, opportunities, or lifestyles with ease.

Action Step:

Pick one area to grow in over the next six months:

- A personal finance course
- A certification in a new field
- A self-help book that challenges your mindset
- A mentor or mastermind group to sharpen your perspective

Lifelong learners are lifelong leaders of their money, their purpose, and their future.

4. Allow Your Values to Lead

Change is not only external it's internal. Your values evolve as you do. The things that once mattered most may take a back seat, while quieter values rise to the surface.

Maybe you now value freedom over fame. Presence over productivity. Impact over income.

Let these values guide your decisions. Your finances, work, and relationships will feel more aligned and your life, more authentic.

Action Step:

Write down your top 3 values right now. Then ask:

- Does my spending reflect these?
- Does my calendar reflect these?
- Does my energy go where I want it to?

If not, it's time to pivot.

Your Financial Plan is a Living Document

Too often, we treat life like a checklist: graduate, get a job, buy a house, save for retirement. But real life is rarely so linear. There are detours, setbacks, awakenings, and new chapters we never expected.

The strongest financial strategy is one that moves with you, not against you.

That means:

- Updating your budget when your lifestyle shifts
- Adjusting your savings goals after a major life event
- Choosing investments that reflect your current risk tolerance and goals

Flexibility keeps you free. And freedom is the ultimate wealth.

Closing Thoughts: Growth Requires Grace

- Give yourself permission to grow, change, and realign.
- There's no shame in shifting direction only strength.
- You're not the same person you were five years ago, and you won't be the same five years from now. That's the beauty of evolution.
- So be gentle with yourself. Embrace your new priorities. Let your financial life reflect your soul's journey not just society's expectations.
- Change isn't something to fear. It's something to shape.
- Stay open. Stay curious. And trust yourself to build a life that evolves beautifully with time.

BUILDING A LEGACY
GIVING BACK AND FINDING PURPOSE
GLOBAL HEALTH,
EDUCATION, POVERTY
LOCAL COMMUNITY
LEADERS
BILL MELINDA
GATES
CHARITY
MENTORSHIP
CHARITY
TRUE WEALTH IS MEASURED NOT BY
WHAT WE HAVE BUT BY THE IMPACT WE MAKE

CHAPTER 7

Building a Legacy, Giving Back and Finding Purpose

What if success wasn't just about what you achieve but about what you contribute?

We often measure wealth by numbers: our bank accounts, homes, or investments. But there comes a point when fulfillment stops growing with your net worth. True satisfaction, the kind that nourishes your soul, often comes not from accumulating more but from sharing what you have.

Legacy isn't just what you leave behind it's how you live now.

And when you use your financial resources to uplift others, you don't just change lives you create meaning.

The True Power of Wealth: Impact Over Income

Take Bill and Melinda Gates. Known for building one of the most successful tech empires in history, they chose to direct their fortune toward solving some of the world's toughest problems: global health, education inequality, and poverty. Through the Gates Foundation, they've saved millions of lives and inspired countless others to think beyond personal gain.

But here's the key:

You don't need billions to make a difference.

Everyday Legacy Builders

Legacy is built not only on a global stage but in everyday communities in coffee shops, classrooms, local food banks, and mentoring circles.

- Think of the retired teacher who tutors neighborhood kids after school.
- The entrepreneur who reinvests profits into scholarships.
- The parent who instills financial wisdom and generosity into their children.

These are the quiet heroes the ones planting seeds for a better future. Their wealth may not be measured in dollars, but in lives touched, hope restored, and dreams made possible.

Impact is not about size. It's about intention.

Ways to Give Back with Purpose

You might be wondering, How do I begin building a legacy?

Start small, but start with heart. Here are ways to give meaningfully:

1. Time The Most Valuable Currency

Sometimes, what people need most isn't money it's mentorship, encouragement, or a listening ear.

- Mentor someone who's just starting their career or business journey.
- Volunteer in your community: schools, shelters, local nonprofits.
- Offer your expertise to those who can't afford it but would deeply benefit.

Time invested in others returns dividends in joy and connection.

2. Talent Share What You Know

We all have unique skills. Teaching someone what you've mastered could open doors they never thought possible.

- Lead a workshop or seminar in your area of expertise.
- Start a blog, podcast, or video series to share your journey and lessons learned.
- Support a young entrepreneur, student, or artist with practical advice.

Knowledge becomes legacy when it's passed on.

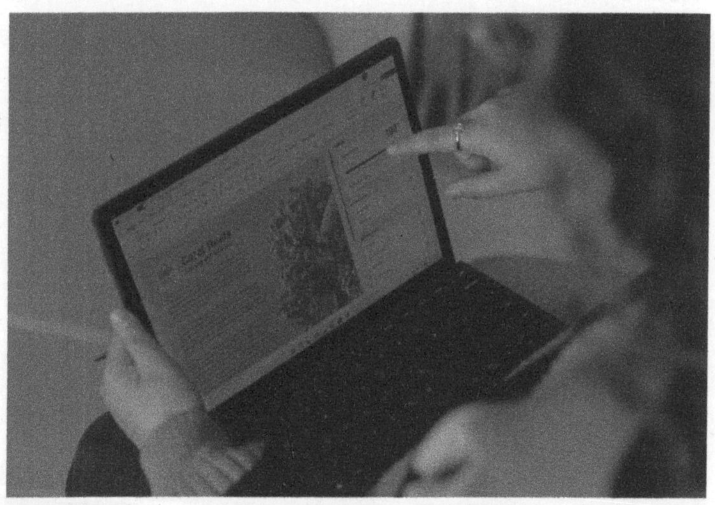

3. Treasure Direct Your Financial Power with Purpose

Whether it's a $10 donation or a $10,000 gift, every contribution matters when it's aligned with your values.

- Support causes that resonate with you: education, clean water, mental health, climate change.
- Create a giving plan: Set aside a percentage of your income each month or year for charitable giving.
- Start something meaningful: a scholarship fund, a nonprofit, a local initiative.

When your money reflects your mission, your legacy becomes an extension of your values.

Why Giving Back Changes You

Giving doesn't just help others it transforms you.

It shifts your mindset from scarcity to abundance, from isolation to connection, from striving to serving.

- Imagine the joy of seeing a mentee land their dream job, or knowing your donation helped build a school in a struggling community. That's not just generosity that's purpose in action.

- You begin to see your wealth not just as security, but as significance.

- Not just what you've earned, but what you're here to do.

Living Legacy: Start Now

You don't need to wait until retirement to begin thinking about legacy. In fact, the best time to start is right now. Because your legacy isn't built in one grand act it's built moment by moment, choice by choice.

Ask yourself:

- What impact do I want to have on the people around me?
- What values do I want to be remembered for?
- How can I use my time, talent, and treasure to create change?

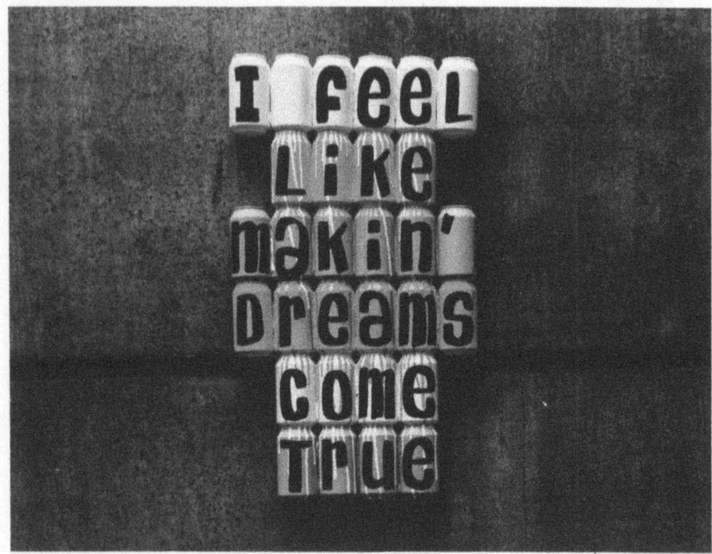

A Ripple Effect of Purpose

One generous act can spark a chain reaction.

- You may inspire someone else to give.
- You may unlock someone's hidden potential.
- You may heal a wound you never knew existed just by showing up, giving, and caring.

That's the ripple effect of living purposefully.

That's what turns success into significance.

In the end, the truest form of wealth is the legacy you leave in people's hearts, not just your will.

- The generosity you live now not the monuments built later.
- The kindness you invest daily not the fortune left untouched.
- You are already powerful. Use it. Share it. Multiply it.
- And build a legacy that lives far beyond your lifetime.

THE ONGOING
JOURNEY TO BALANCE
BOUNDARIES
REST
RELATIONSHIPS
PURPOSE
PURPOSE
Physical • Mental • Emotional • Spiritual
Inner peace • Resilience
LIVING A BALANCED LIFE
IS A JOURNEY

CONCLUSION

The Ongoing Journey to Balance

Living a balanced life means nurturing every aspect of your well-being: physical, mental, emotional, and spiritual. It's about more than just juggling responsibilities; it's about thriving in all areas of your life.

Boundaries: Setting clear boundaries is essential. It allows you to prioritize what truly matters, whether that's work, family, or personal time. Remember, saying "no" can be just as powerful as saying "yes."

Make time for rest and relationships. In our fast paced world, we often overlook the importance of downtime and connection. Schedule regular breaks and invest in your relationships. Quality time with loved ones fuels our emotional health and brings joy to our lives.

Purpose: Maintaining a sense of purpose is crucial for long-term happiness. Reflect on what drives you, your passions, your goals, and your values. When you align your daily actions with your purpose, you cultivate fulfillment.

Inner peace and resilience are byproducts of a balanced life. When you nurture all aspects of yourself, you build the strength to navigate life's challenges with grace. It's not about perfection; it's about harmony.

So, how do we achieve this balance? Start small. Incorporate little changes into your routine, meditate for five minutes a day, take a walk in nature, or dedicate time each week to a hobby you love.

Remember, living a balanced life is a journey, not a destination. Embrace the process and celebrate your progress along the way. Focus on finding harmony in the different areas of your life, and watch as your overall well-being flourishes.

CLOSING STORY

I've officially retired from fighting professionally. It wasn't an easy decision, there are still days when I feel the urge to compete, but that chapter of my life has come to a close.

Letting go of the constant focus on boxing has allowed me to find balance in other areas of my life. I've discovered new priorities and joys that I once overlooked. These days, I feel a deep sense of relief and contentment. I wake up with gratitude and a world full of opportunity.

Boxing is still close to my heart. Now, I give back by sharing my knowledge and experiences with the next generation. Helping others chase their dreams and passions brings me a new kind of satisfaction, one that goes beyond personal achievement.

Living through an unbalanced life has taught me valuable lessons. I've seen firsthand how focusing too much on one thing no matter how meaningful can lead to stress, anxiety, and even depression. I truly believe that kind of imbalance can be unhealthy. That's why I'm passionate about guiding others toward a more grounded, well-rounded path.

Be Published